GLACIER

BY
Phyllis Root

I wish to thank Michelle Rotter, Public Information Officer at Glacier National Park, and Paul Tackes, Seasonal Ranger/Naturalist at Sequoia National Park, for all their help. Any mistakes are my own.

PUBLISHED BY
CRESTWOOD HOUSE
Mankato, MN, U.S.A.

LIBRARY OF CONGRESS CATALOGING IN PUBLICATION DATA

Root, Phyllis.
　Glacier

(National parks)
Includes index.
SUMMARY: Describes the geography, wildlife, and history of Glacier National Park.
　1. Glacier National Park (Mont.) — Juvenile literature. [1. Glacier National Park (Mont.) 2. National parks and reserves.] I. Title. II.
Series: National Parks (Mankato, Minn.)
F737.G5R64　　　　　1988　　　　917.86'52—dc19　　　　　　　88-18945
ISBN 0-89686-408-1

International Standard Book Number: 0-89686-408-1	Library of Congress Catalog Card Number: 88-18945

PHOTO CREDITS

Cover: Paul Tackes
Paul Tackes: 4, 8-9, 10, 12-13, 15, 16-17, 20, 26, 27, 29, 30, 32-33, 39
Tom Stack & Associates: (Tom Algire) 7, 18-19, 40; (Ann & Myron Sutton) 23; (Kevin Magee) 24-25; (Thomas Kitchin) 34; (Wendy Shattil & Robert Rozinski) 37
Journalism Services: (Dave Brown) 42

Produced by Carnival Enterprises.

CRESTWOOD HOUSE

Box 3427, Mankato, MN, U.S.A. 56002

TABLE OF CONTENTS

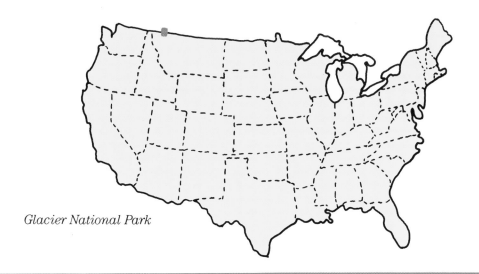

Glacier National Park

THE SHINING MOUNTAINS

Up from the prairie the mountains rise, startling and magnificent. The first explorers who saw them called them the "shining mountains." The Blackfeet tribes called them the "backbone of the world." Today they are part of Glacier National Park, a wild and beautiful corner of Montana.

Even in summer ice and snow sparkle on the mountain peaks. Some of the snow has packed and hardened into glaciers. But the park is not named for these small glaciers. It is named for the great rivers of ice that once covered the mountains. These huge glaciers carved out sharp peaks, high ridges, and deep valleys.

In this rough country, waterfalls tumble down cliffs. Mountain goats and bighorn sheep leap and scramble over rocks. Moose and mule deer feed in the forests and lakes. Grizzly bears roam free.

Winter in Glacier can end in July and start again in August. Columbian ground squirrels sleep nine months of the year snug in the earth under the snow. In the spring, avalanches roar down the valleys. Summer scatters wildflowers over the land. In autumn, bald eagles gather to feast on salmon in McDonald Creek.

Glacier National Park is 1,500 square miles of wilderness. It is a land of rock and water, prairie, forest, and *tundra.* Most of all, it is a land of wild and breathtaking beauty.

Glacier National Park is named after the huge glaciers that carved out sharp peaks and deep valleys.

FROM OCEAN FLOOR TO MOUNTAIN PEAK

Glacier's rocks and mountains tell an ancient story.

A billion years ago the mountains of Glacier did not exist. A flat, shallow sea covered the land. Sand and mud settled at the bottom of the sea. More and more layers built up over millions of years. Some were red, some green, some tan. The weight of all those layers turned the lower layers into rock. Some rocks still hold the print of raindrops that fell millions of years ago. Even ripples in the mud and sand of that ancient sea bottom hardened into stone.

Underneath the sea, volcanoes squeezed up hot, melted rock. In some places the hot rock cooled between layers of stone. In other places it cooled underwater and made puffy pillow shapes.

Seventy-five million years ago, the earth began to wrinkle. The land rose and folded. Over millions of years, the "wrinkles" became what are now the Rocky Mountains. These mountains stretch from Canada, through Glacier National Park, down to New Mexico. Glacier has two mountain ranges. The Livingston Range is on the west, and the Lewis Range is on the east.

The earth did more than wrinkle in Glacier. A huge block of rock about 30 miles long broke loose. This block slid slowly east for almost 40 miles. As it slid, it tilted. After millions of years, this very old rock from deep in the earth came to rest on top of younger rocks. This is called the *Lewis Overthrust.* It runs along the eastern edge of the park.

Bands of color can be seen on the mountainsides. These are the different layers of rock that formed on the sea bottom millions of years ago. Pebbles from these layers color the stream beds throughout the park.

RIVERS OF ICE

Glacier's valleys and mountains were once buried in ice and snow. Three million years ago only the highest peaks showed above a blanket of white. Snow fell in winter faster than it could melt in summer. The snow and ice packed together tighter and tighter. The layers piled up thousands of feet

FUN FACT The highest peak in Glacier National Park is Mount Cleveland. It is 10,448 feet high.

Beautiful, colored pebbles are found in stream beds throughout the park.

Glaciers wore away a mountain to form the knife-edged ridge of The Garden Wall.

deep. Finally they were so heavy they began to slide down the mountainsides. These moving masses of ice and snow were *glaciers*. Down the mountains and through the valleys the glaciers crept.

The glaciers plucked up rocks and boulders and carried them along. They scraped away the soil and left scratches in the hard bedrock underneath.

Where they rested against the mountains, the glaciers carved huge hollows in the mountainsides called *cirques*. In places they scooped out basins for lakes. When they wore away a mountain from two sides they carved a knife-edged ridge called an *arete*. The Garden Wall in Glacier National Park is an arete. It is so thin at the top that the sun shines through a hole in it.

When glaciers scraped away at three sides of a mountain they carved a *horn.* Reynolds Mountain, with its three steep sides, is a horn.

Sometimes glaciers carved through the mountain from opposite sides. Logan Pass on Going-to-the-Sun Road is a place where the glaciers met.

Before the glaciers came, rivers had cut V-shaped valleys into the earth. The glaciers widened and deepened these valleys. They flattened the floors and steepened the walls, making the valleys U-shaped.

When the glaciers finally melted, they left piles of rocks and soil called

Reynolds Mountain is a "horn" formed when glaciers scraped away three of its sides.

moraines. If a moraine blocked up a stream it made a lake. Josephine Lake, like many lakes in the park, was formed by a moraine.

At least four times in the past three million years, glaciers moved over the land and then melted. Today there are nearly 50 small glaciers in the park. But these glaciers are not part of those ancient glaciers. They began to form after the end of the last great Ice Age. They still scrape away at the earth. But the changes they make are small. It was the giant ice rivers of long ago that left their mark everywhere in Glacier National Park.

THE FIRST PEOPLE

No one knows who first crossed the mountains of Glacier or camped beside its rivers. Many tribes of Native Americans have lived near what is now the park. The first white explorers found the Blackfeet living on the eastern plains. But others lived there before the Blackfeet. The Kalispel, the Kootenai, the Stony, and the Flathead tribes had all lived on the prairie. They hunted elk, deer, antelope, and *bison* (large, shaggy animals often called buffalo).

For many years the Blackfeet hunted with bows and arrows. Dogs helped them haul their belongings from camp to camp. But in the 1700s, the Blackfeet began to use guns and horses. They moved toward the Rocky Mountains, driving the other tribes west.

These other tribes moved into the mountains and valleys. They learned to fish and hunt mountain sheep and goats. But they still crossed the mountains several times a year to hunt bison.

The huge herds of bison that roamed the prairie were very important to the Native American tribes. They ate bison meat. From bison skins they made warm robes, moccasins, and coverings for their tepee homes. But life began to change for the tribes because of another animal—the beaver.

IN SEARCH OF WEALTH

In the early 1800s, fur trappers came to the Rocky Mountains. They wanted to trade with the Native Americans for beaver skins. Hats made from

FUN FACT   Glacier ice looks white when it is covered with snow or when you
see it from a long way away. But up close the ice of a glacier is really blue.   11

A stream blocked by a "moraine" formed Josephine Lake.

13

beaver skins were in fashion. Fur companies built trading posts west of the mountains. But the fierce Blackfeet kept the traders out of the eastern mountains.

In time fashion changed. Beaver hats were no longer in demand. But the Blackfeet changed, too. A deadly disease called smallpox killed over 60,000 of them. Soldiers attacked a peaceful camp of Blackfeet in 1870, killing 173 men, women, and children. Weakened by disease, attacked by soldiers, the Blackfeet could no longer protect their lands.

Trading posts opened. They traded goods and whiskey for bison hides. Whites and Native Americans killed the bison for their skins. The great herds vanished.

In 1895, the government bought the eastern side of the mountains from the Blackfeet. The land was opened for mining. Prospectors searched for gold and copper. They staked claims and dug mines at places like Cracker Lake and Josephine Lake. But there was little wealth in the mines.

Some people drilled for gas and oil. One prospector found enough gas to heat and light his home for seven years. But no one got rich. The wells, like the mines, were abandoned.

In 1889, the Great Northern Railroad explored a pass that cut through the mountains. In 1891, the railroad crossed the mountains at Marias Pass. It brought hunters and tourists. People settled in the Flathead Valley and around Lake McDonald.

THE CROWN OF THE CONTINENT

Not everyone wanted to get rich from the mountains. A few people wanted a national park. George Bird Grinnell wrote about the beauty of the mountains. He called them "the crown of the continent." Grinnell thought they should be saved for all people to enjoy.

By 1897, the mountains were part of a forest reserve. But people could still hunt, mine, cut timber, graze cattle, and build homes in a forest reserve. The mountains needed more protection.

James Hill was president of the Great Northern Railroad. Hill wanted a

FUN FACT The Great Northern Railroad adopted the Rocky Mountain goat for its trademark. This railroad no longer exists, but some railroad cars still have a picture of a Rocky Mountain goat on them.

park, too. With his help, a bill was introduced into Congress. For two-and-a-half years, Congress studied the bill. Some homesteaders were afraid a park would take away their land. Some people felt land should be used, not preserved. Finally an agreement was reached.

On May 11, 1910, President Taft signed the bill. A million acres of wilderness became Glacier National Park.

In 1910 a million acres of wilderness became Glacier National Park.

Going-to-the-Sun Road is a 50-mile road cut through the middle of Glacier National Park.

BUILDING A PARK

Once Glacier became a park, changes began. Trails were laid out. The railroad helped build five chalets and Many Glacier Hotel.

In 1933, Going-to-the-Sun Road opened. This 50-mile road cut through

the heart of the park. It took 12 years to build. Building the road was hard work. Workers were lowered down the mountainside with ropes. They placed dynamite charges in the rock. Over half of the road was blasted out of solid rock. When the road was done, people could drive through the magnificent mountains.

Breathtaking scenery greets hikers who follow the Highline Trail.

These mountains do not end at the border. North of Glacier in Canada is Waterton Lakes National Park. It has the same stunning mountains carved by ice. In 1932, the United States and Canada joined their two parks into one. The Waterton-Glacier International Peace Park is a symbol of friendship between the two countries.

WHAT'S IN A NAME?

Glacier's history can be read in the names of its mountains, rivers, lakes, and valleys. Some Native American names have been changed. But many places still have names given them by the Blackfeet and other tribes.

Mountains like Red Eagle and Heavy Runner were named for tribal leaders. Pitamakan Pass was named for a famous warrior maiden who led war parties across the pass.

Wild Goose Island in St. Mary Lake was named after a pair of geese that nested there.

Stoney Indian Pass, Stoney Indian Lake, and Stoney Indian Peak are named after the Stoney tribe. These people were called Stoney because they cooked their food with heated rocks.

Once two tribes built medicine lodges on the shores of a lake. This lake became Two Medicine Lake.

Some places in the park are named for early explorers. Grinnell Glacier was named for George Bird Grinnell. Cracker Lake may have gotten its name from some prospectors who left part of their lunch behind at the lake, including crackers.

Some names come from animals. Wild Goose Island is a small, rocky island in St. Mary Lake. It is named for a pair of geese that nested there for many years.

One story about Medicine Grizzly Peak tells about a huge grizzly. This bear once roamed Cut Bank Canyon. The Blackfeet believed it had great medicine, or special power. Its footprints were 13 inches long and 7 inches wide at the toe. A lion hunter named Chance Beebe finally tracked and killed the grizzly. Medicine Grizzly Lake and Medicine Grizzly Peak are named for this legendary bear.

BACKBONE OF THE WORLD

The mountains of the park are part of the *Continental Divide*. What the mountains "divide" is water. Rain or snow that falls on the western side of the mountains ends up in the Pacific Ocean. On the eastern side, it winds up in the Atlantic Ocean.

In Glacier National Park, the west and east sides of the mountains are like two different worlds. One side is damp, the other side is dry. This happens because clouds blow across the land from west to east. The mountains are high enough to catch these clouds. As the clouds climb up the mountain, they cool off. Their load of rain or snow falls. Cedar and hemlock forests, dense and damp, grow on the western slopes in Glacier. The wind blowing down the eastern side of the mountain dries the land. The eastern slopes are rocky and drier, stretching down to the prairie.

Sometimes in winter a warm wind blows down the eastern slopes, melting the snow. This is a *chinook* wind. The Blackfeet called it a "snow-eater." A chinook can uncover grass for animals to eat. Not all chinooks are warm, though. Klondike chinooks that blow down from the Arctic can be cold and fierce.

One mountain in Glacier is called Triple Divide Peak. Water flows from it in three different directions. Some water ends up in the Atlantic Ocean. Some flows to the Pacific. Some water finds its way north to Hudson Bay. Three raindrops falling on this mountain could end up in oceans thousands of miles apart.

THE PRAIRIE

Most of Glacier National Park is made of mountains. But along the eastern edge of the park the short-grass prairie pushes up against the mountains.

Huge herds of bison, sometimes four million to a herd, once waded through the seas of grass. Now only small, protected herds remain. Deer, elk, and grizzly find food in the prairie. Mountain lions stalk mule deer. Badgers burrow under the earth. In the spring, blue camas, purple asters, and yellow sunflowers bloom in the short grass.

IN THE FORESTS

Trees cover almost two-thirds of the park. But the forests of Glacier are not all the same. Sun, rain, wind, snow, soil, and fire all help shape a forest.

Western red cedar and hemlock trees thrive in the heavy rains that fall on the western slopes. Western red cedar trees grow tall and wide. The largest western red cedar in the park is 100 feet high. These trees may grow for hundreds of years.

Moss covers logs and rocks in the forest. Green ferns uncurl, and white trillums bloom. But shade from the dense trees keeps most flowers and shrubs from growing. Animals that eat plants, grasses, berries, and roots find little food in the cedar and hemlock forest. Squirrels live here. Woodpeckers hammer at the trees. But this forest is not home for many large animals.

Sometimes fires burn a forest down. If that happens, lodgepole pines will probably grow from the ashes. Their seeds sprout and grow in bright, open sunlight. The heat from a fire even helps lodgepole pine cones open so they can release their seeds.

FUN FACT In 1972, a klondike chinook from Alaska hit a freight train near the park. The wind knocked seven flat cars off the tracks.

But as lodgepole pines grow tall, they shade the ground. Their own seedlings cannot survive in the shade. Other trees that can live in shade begin to sprout beneath the lodgepole pines. Slowly, a new forest takes root.

It may be a forest of spruce and fir trees. Here mule deer, black bear, spruce grouse, and other animals all find food.

The western larch is common on the west side of Glacier National Park. Its bark is so thick it can often survive a fire. Like a pine tree, the larch has needles. Most pine trees keep their needles all year. But each fall larches turn bright yellow, painting the hills with color. Then their needles fall off. A forest of larches in winter may look like a stand of dead trees. But in spring new green needles cover the branches.

The forests of Glacier National Park offer food and shelter to a variety of animals.

Trees cover almost two-thirds of Glacier National Park.

Glacier lilies blooming in the alpine meadows are a beautiful sight.

HIGH COUNTRY

High in the mountains the trees are twisted and small. In the wind and cold of the high country they grow slowly. A 100-year-old tree may be only ten feet tall. Often the trees are bare of branches a short way above the ground. Branches close to the ground are protected by snow. But icy winds snap off branches above the snow.

Higher still, the forest ends. This is the *alpine* country—rocks and cliffs, snowfields and glaciers. Snow can fall any month of the year. Many places are covered with snow late in July. In this harsh land, alpine plants have found ways to survive. Some grow in clumps, hugging the ground. Glacier lilies bloom even through the snow.

For a few brief weeks of summer, the alpine meadows blossom with color.

FUN FACT Over 60 mammals, 200 birds, and 1,200 different plants are found in Glacier National Park.

The Hanging Gardens at Logan Pass are a splendor of flowers. Yellow glacier lilies and buttercups are followed by pink shooting stars, white dryas, purple asters, and blue gentians. Where water melts and flows out of glaciers, red and yellow monkey flowers bloom. But the splendor is brief. Winter soon locks up the land again.

Sheep and goats spend the summer high on the slopes. When winter threatens, they move lower down. The *ptarmigan* (pronounced TAR-mi-gan) is one of the only animals that lives all year round in the alpine country. It keeps warm by fluffing up its feathers or burrowing into the snow.

UP ON THE ICE

Today there are nearly 50 small glaciers in the park. Sperry Glacier, one of the largest, covers about 300 acres. But in the early 1900s, there were 90

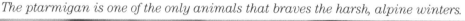

The ptarmigan is one of the only animals that braves the harsh, alpine winters.

glaciers. Sperry Glacier covered over 800 acres. What happened to the glaciers? Where did they go?

Between 1900 and 1950, the glaciers began to melt. Many disappeared. Some of the bigger glaciers split into several small glaciers. Some glaciers shrank until they were too small to move. They became *icefields*. An icefield looks like a glacier, but it never moves.

Since 1950, the melting has slowed down. The glaciers are still shrinking. They are shrinking very slowly, however. They are still some of the largest glaciers in the United States' Rocky Mountains.

Some of the park's glaciers can be seen from the road. But seeing a glacier up close means hiking to get to one. Being on a glacier can be like walking in another world. Streams flow across the snow. Rocks perch on cones of ice. Water running under the ice hollows out tunnels and caves.

A visit to a glacier can be a risky trip. As a glacier moves over humps in the earth, large, dangerous cracks called *crevasses* can open in the ice. Even in summer, snow may hide a crevasse. But the snow can give way underfoot. A person who falls into a crevasse can suffocate or freeze. The safest way to visit a glacier is with a ranger-naturalist. No one should ever go up on a glacier alone.

FALLING WATER

A thousand waterfalls splash over the rocks in Glacier National Park. Water leaps from ledge to ledge down stairstep falls. Some waterfalls, like Birdwoman Falls, plunge from *hanging valleys*. These are smaller valleys that once ran into larger ones. Glaciers carved the larger valleys deeper than the smaller ones. When the ice melted, the smaller valleys were left "hanging" high above the deeper valley floor.

At Running Eagle Falls water runs over the top of the falls. It also flows from an opening halfway down the cliff. In summer, the river is shallow, and water flows only from the lower opening. But when the river runs high with melted snow, water pours from both falls.

Partway down Piegan Mountain, water flows out of the side of the rock. This water is probably from Piegan Glacier. The glacier lies on the other side of the mountain. Melted ice and snow from the glacier run down through layers of rock in the mountain until they flow out the other side.

Hikers must keep an eye out for large, dangerous cracks that form in the ice.

Many *ouzels* (pronounced OO-zels) make their homes near waterfalls. These small, grey birds often build their nests out of living moss. Spray from waterfalls keeps the nests moist. When the baby birds are ready to leave the nest, they tumble down into the water. Soon they are flying into the stream like their parents and walking along the stream bottom to eat the insects they find there.

LAKES THE GLACIERS LEFT BEHIND

More than 200 lakes sparkle in the sun of Glacier National Park. They were formed when the glaciers moved over the land and then melted.

Shrinking glaciers sometimes left large chunks of ice behind. These chunks melted and became "pothole" lakes. Sometimes the gravel and sand that washed out of a melting glacier formed a dam. The water behind the dam became a lake. Bowman Lake, Kintla Lake, and Elizabeth Lake were dammed up by melting glaciers.

Iceberg Lake lies in a cirque a mile across. The lake was named for the icebergs that broke off from a glacier. Sometimes the lake is frozen over until July. Even when it thaws, islands of ice still float in the lake. The water is always cold. No fish live in it.

Once as a joke some fisherman caught a trout in another lake and covered it with fur. They claimed they had caught the fur-covered trout in Iceberg Lake. Newspapers across the country ran pictures of this "rare" fish before they found out they had been tricked.

Many lakes get their color from glaciers. The color comes from rocks that the glacier grinds into a fine powder called *rock flour*. This powder washes out of the melting glaciers. Large amounts of rock flour color lakes and streams a greenish white. Smaller amounts of rock flour turn lakes like Cracker Lake a deep turquoise.

Over a thousand waterfalls tumble through Glacier National Park.

"Rock flour" washes into Glacier's lakes and turns them a beautiful green.

A mother bear protecting her cubs is the most dangerous bear of all.

WARNING: BEAR COUNTRY

The grizzly bear is king of the mountains in Glacier National Park. Once these bears roamed over much of the continent. But the settlers that moved west hunted and killed grizzlies. Now these bears live mainly in Canada and Alaska. Glacier National Park is one of the last refuges for grizzly bears in the United States. About 200 grizzlies live in and around the park.

Many grizzly bears have white-tipped fur. This gives them a "grizzled" look. That is how they got their name. Grizzlies have a powerful hump of shoulder muscle. Their long, sharp claws are good for digging, fighting, and pulling things apart. Their senses of hearing and smell are very keen. Grizzlies can run as fast as 45 miles per hour for a short time. No person can outrun a grizzly.

FUN FACT Grizzly bears have been seen sliding down snow banks and climbing back up to slide down over and over again.

Grizzly bears eat almost anything—berries, grubs, dead animals, grass, honey, nuts. They may roam over thousands of acres searching for food. They sleep in dens most of the winter. The cubs, usually twins, are born in the winter den.

Black bears also live in the park. They are smaller than grizzlies, and their noses are more pointed. A black bear has no hump on its back. Like grizzlies, black bears can be many different colors. They eat mostly berries, nuts, bulbs, and insects. Black bears are tree-climbers. Most full-grown grizzlies are too heavy to climb trees.

Bears can be very dangerous. A mother bear protecting her cubs is the most dangerous bear of all. A grizzly can kill a person with one swipe of its paw. Since Glacier became a park, grizzlies have killed eight people. On August 13, 1967, two women were killed by two different bears on the same night.

These bears had been eating from garbage dumps in the park. Usually bears avoid people who do not threaten them. But these grizzlies had lost their fear of humans. They had learned that people and food go together. Now the park is careful to keep all garbage away from bears.

Campers in the park must also be careful. They must keep campsites clean. All food should be stored in the trunks of cars with the windows closed. Backcountry campers are required to hang food from trees to keep it away from bears. No one should ever bury food or store it in a tent.

Once a bear learns that humans mean food, it will keep coming to people to eat. The bear will no longer be wild. One day it may injure or kill someone. Then the bear will have to be killed, too.

Bears need a lot of room to live. Only the mountains of Wyoming, Idaho, and Montana are still empty enough for grizzly bears. For the grizzlies of Glacier to survive, they must be protected from people.

A FEAST FOR EAGLES

Every fall hundreds of bald eagles gather at McDonald Creek. They come to eat the thousands of dark red salmon swimming up the creek to lay their eggs. Eagles have keen eyesight and sharp, curved claws with tiny spikes. They can catch and hold a slippery fish with these claws. The eagles wait in the trees along the creek to swoop down and snatch the fish. Then they fly back to the trees to eat their catch.

Younger eagles often wade out into the creek to pick up dead fish. The younger eagles are all brown. They do not have white heads and tails until they are several years old.

Only a few of the eagles who come to the creek live in the park. Most of the eagles come from Canada. They are on their way to winter homes in Idaho, Washington, Colorado, Nevada, Oregon, and Montana. They come to Glacier to eat fish and store up energy for the long flight.

The eagles begin to gather in September. They come just before sunrise. The birds do most of their feeding early in the morning or late in the afternoon. Each eagle eats about six fish a day. Right before sunset they fly off to their roosts. November is the best time to see eagles. By December they are gone.

The biggest threat to eagles today is losing the land where they live. By cutting trees and building new suburbs and towns, people are destroying the places where eagles nest and feed. Wild places like Glacier give the eagle a chance to survive.

MOUNTAIN CLIMBERS

High on the slopes of Glacier, Rocky Mountain goats and bighorn sheep graze and leap. These are the mountain climbers of the park.

Rocky Mountain goats live on the mountains above the trees winter and summer. Each of their feet has a spongy pad in the center of the hoof. This pad helps their feet cling to the rocks. They can use every tiny crack and knob for climbing. Their thick, shaggy coats keep them warm even in winter. They use their pointed black horns to defend themselves.

Early in June nanny goats will have one kid each. Often a nanny, her new kid, and her two-year-old kid stay together in their own small herd. Gunsight Pass and Swiftcurrent Lake are good places to watch for mountain goats.

Bighorn sheep also graze high on the mountains in summer. The females, or ewes, range lower on the slopes than the rams. In the fall the rams come down the mountains and fight. With lowered heads two rams charge each other. The clash of their curved horns rings through the valleys. Again and again they crash horn to horn. Finally one ram will give up and go away. Bighorn sheep can often be seen in the winter around the Many Glacier area.

FUN FACT   An eagle can see a small animal moving in the grass from a mile away.

An eagle's nest can be 8 feet wide, 20 feet deep, and weigh 4,000 pounds.

Rocky Mountain goats have a spongy pad in the center of each hoof that helps their feet cling to the rocks.

CALL OF THE WOLF

Wolves once roamed over the mountains and valleys of Glacier National Park. But they were driven out of the Rocky Mountains. Cattle ranchers were afraid wolves would eat their cattle. They shot or poisoned thousands of wolves. Government trappers hunted down the rest. By the 1930s, there were no wolves left in the Rocky Mountains of the United States. For many years the call of the wolf has been silent in Glacier.

Now wolves are beginning to return. In 1985, a pack of grey wolves moved south into the park from Canada. The next year a litter of wolf pups was born within the park. Wolves now live near the North Fork of the Flathead River on the park's west side. On the east side they live near the St. Mary area. They are very shy of people.

FUN FACT Moose often feed in a pond with their whole heads underwater. Only their ears stick up above water, listening for danger.

Grey wolves are not always grey. They can be many colors—grey, tan, black, or white. Wolves weigh up to 100 pounds. They usually live in packs of a male, a female, and their young. One way they communicate with each other is by howling.

Wolves are predators. This means they hunt and eat other animals. Wolves often kill animals that are old, sick, or weak. Without any natural enemies like the wolf, a herd of elk or deer could grow too large. If there is not enough food for them, many would starve.

LAND IN BLOOM

In the spring, streams run cold with melting snow. Bears wake up and bring their cubs out of the den. Wildflowers begin to bloom low on the mountains. By July and August the hillsides are a blaze of color. Over 100 kinds of wildflowers may be blooming at the same time in the park.

High on the mountains the growing season is so short that all the plants flower at once. They must hurry before snow covers the ground again. There is so little time for growing that some plants take several years just to blossom. The first year these plants may shoot up. The next year they have flowers. The third year the plants produce seeds. It takes them three years to do what most plants do in one summer.

In the spring, beargrass is close behind the melting snow, chasing spring up the mountainside. Beargrass is a lily, not a grass. Bears do not eat it, although goats do. It got its name when an explorer saw some grizzlies walking through the flowers and named the plant beargrass. Some years only a few plants bloom. Other years the large white flowers cover the slopes.

ON THE TRAIL

Glacier is a park for hikers. More than 700 miles of trails lead to beaver ponds, forests, alpine meadows, and waterfalls. Hikers see the beauty of the wilderness up close.

The hike to Avalanche Lake passes through a cedar forest where ferns and queencup beadlilies grow.

The appearance of the beargrass plant is one of the first signs of spring in the mountains.

Hikers can enjoy colorful Indian paintbrush plants that bloom among the rocks in the alpine meadows.

The trail to Cracker Lake leads past snowberry bushes. It ends at the bright waters of Cracker Lake. Old mining equipment can still be seen there.

Highline Trail from Logan Pass leads past alpine meadows. Yellow columbine and Indian paintbrush bloom among the rocks. Hikers may see mountain goats, bighorn sheep, or even a grizzly.

Hikers should learn how long or difficult a trail is before hiking it. Some trails are rugged and rough; others are blocked by snow. All trails pass through bear country. Rangers may close a trail if bears have been seen on it. Hikers should check with a ranger to see if a trail is open and safe.

THE LONG, WHITE WINTER

By September, frost lies on the ground. The peaks of many mountains may already be covered with snow. For much of the year, winter holds the land in its icy grip.

Winter temperatures can drop to –40°F. Hundreds of inches of snow can cover the ground. Snowdrifts on Going-to-the-Sun Road may be 80 feet deep.

Yet even in the snow and cold, animals survive. Some animals spend the winter in homes under the snow. Bears sleep in their dens. Marmots *hibernate.* Their heartbeats slow and their body temperatures drop to just above freezing. For these animals the summer is spent getting ready for winter. They must eat enough food to last them through their long, cold sleep. A marmot ready to hibernate in autumn is so fat its belly drags on the ground. While it hibernates its body slowly uses up this stored food.

Some animals do not sleep the winter away. The *pika,* a small animal with short ears and legs, does not hibernate. During the summer it gathers grass and herbs into huge piles. These piles dry into hay. When snow covers everything, the pika tunnels underneath to its stores of hay. Beneath the snow it survives with its winter food.

Many animals change to winter dress. The weasel and snowshoe hare have white fur in the winter months. The ptarmigan's feathers turn white. This makes it harder for enemies to see these animals.

Snow protects many animals by trapping their heat to help them keep warm. But too much snow can harm animals such as deer. In deep snow they cannot search for food or run from their enemies.

Winter can be both harsh and beautiful in Glacier. In the snowy silence the earth holds her breath, waiting for spring.

FLOODS, FIRES, AND AVALANCHES

The face of Glacier National Park changes slowly. Glaciers grow and shrink away. Water cuts through rock inch by slow inch. But in some ways

Many people each year come to enjoy Glacier National Park's beauty and wildness.

the land changes suddenly.

Snow can melt so quickly in the spring that it floods the rivers, washing away trees, dirt, and animals. Many streams are littered with boulders, logs, and dead trees tossed there by flood waters.

Fire can change the land, too. Forest fires burn away the trees. New forests begin to grow from the ashes. Meadow flowers, shrubs, and small trees grow in the burned-over land. These become food for moose and deer.

Even in winter, when the world seems frozen, the land is still changing. Ice breaks tiny pieces of rock apart to make new soil. Snow may thunder down the mountain in an *avalanche,* uprooting trees and heaving boulders around. Sometimes animals are caught by the roaring snow. Their dead bodies are an important source of food for grizzlies when the bears first wake in the spring.

FUN FACT Avalanches have been clocked as fast as 157 miles an hour.

Some mountain slopes are avalanche paths. Snow builds up and crashes down year after year. Trees have no chance to grow here. The shrubs and small plants that do grow are food for elk, deer, and moose.

A DELICATE BALANCE

Glacier is rough and wild. But its wilderness is delicate, too. The borders of the park cannot keep out everything that threatens it. One of the greatest dangers is people, both inside and outside the park.

People come to Glacier to see its beauty and wildness. But people tramping over an alpine meadow can destroy years of slow growth. People feeding wild animals will teach these animals to come to humans for food. Sometimes the animals forget how to find food for themselves. When winter comes, they may starve.

Some animals, like grizzlies, do not stay in the park. Their range goes beyond its borders. Once outside the park the bears are not protected. Plans for oil drilling and logging outside the park threaten land the grizzly calls home. Humans and bears do not mix. If the grizzlies lose too much of their range, they may not be able to survive in the park.

Even mining outside the park may pollute the air and water inside the park.

The world needs wilderness. Animals need it to survive undisturbed by people. Native plants need their native earth to grow.

People need wilderness, too. They need a place to heal their spirits, a place to sense the power of the earth. But Glacier may not be wild forever. If the grizzly disappears and the lakes and air are polluted, losing the wilderness will touch us all.

IF YOU GO

There are many things to see and do in Glacier National Park. Here are a few ideas:

Take a hike with a ranger to see a glacier.

Fish in a mountain lake.

Hike Huckleberry Mountain Trail to see how fire has a part in the life of a forest.

Hike Trail of the Cedars to Avalanche Gorge.

Follow Swiftcurrent Lake Nature Trail around the lake.

Look for goats at the Hanging Gardens near Logan Pass.

Take a boat ride on St. Mary Lake. At the end of the boat ride, hike with a ranger to see St. Mary Falls.

Hear a ranger-naturalist give a campfire talk.

Visit a historic ranger station.

Drive through the mountains on Going-to-the-Sun Road.

TAKING CARE

Glacier National Park is the home of grizzlies and eagles, arctic willows and beargrass. People are visitors in the park. They must be careful not to harm it. They must also be careful not to hurt themselves. Wilderness can be dangerous. It is important to know the rules and follow them.

Never climb, hike, or go up on a glacier alone. The best way to see a glacier is with a ranger-naturalist. When you are on a glacier, be careful of crevasses. A fall into a crevasse can be dangerous.

Remember that bears live here. Wear bear bells, or make noise when you hike. This could give a bear a chance to hear you coming and get out of the way.

If a bear comes toward you, get off the trail and lie face down. Cover the back of your neck with your hands. Don't run from a grizzly—it would probably chase you.

Hikers should wear long pants, long sleeves, and carry insect repellant.

Carry fresh drinking water with you. Don't drink right from a stream. The water could make you sick.

If you backpack, hike, or climb, carry warm clothes, rain gear, matches, and extra food. Storms can come up suddenly in the mountains.

If you plan to climb a mountain or go into the backcountry, you must register with a ranger before you go and when you come back. You will need a permit to camp in the backcountry.

If you camp out, keep yourself and your campsite clean. Food attracts bears. Hang your food high in a tree away from camp. Don't take food into

FUN FACT Glacier National Park is larger than the whole state of Rhode Island.

your tent. Carry out your garbage—don't bury it.

Fires are not allowed in many areas. Check with a ranger to see if fires are allowed where you are going.

If lightning is anywhere in the sky, go lower down the mountain.

Don't go on or near snow banks. They can collapse suddenly. If you were to start sliding down a snow bank, you might not be able to stop.

Never try to get close to animals or feed them, even if they look harmless. They are wild animals, and they should stay wild.

Don't go swimming in the park's streams and rivers. Currents can be stronger than they look, and the water is very cold.

Pets must be kept on leashes in campsites. They are not allowed in the backcountry.

If you plan to ski in Glacier, learn about avalanches. It could save your life.

Stay on the trails. Walking across the alpine meadow can destroy plants that took years to grow. Leave the plants, flowers, rocks, and pine cones for everyone to enjoy.

FOR MORE PARK INFORMATION

For more information about Glacier National Park, write to:

Superintendent
Glacier National Park
West Glacier, MT 59936

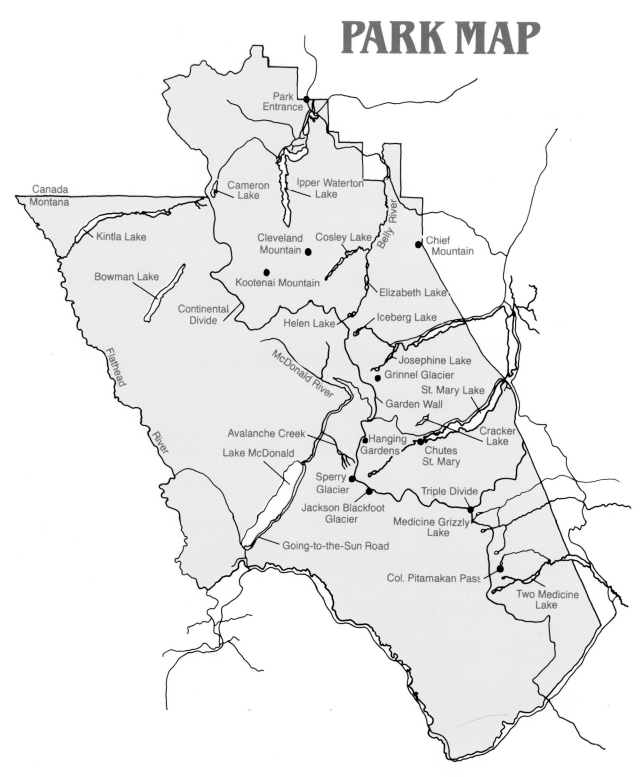

PARK MAP

Park Entrance

Canada
Montana

Cameron Lake

Ipper Waterton Lake

Belly River

Kintla Lake

Cleveland Mountain

Cosley Lake

Chief Mountain

Bowman Lake

Kootenai Mountain

Elizabeth Lake

Continental Divide

Helen Lake

Iceberg Lake

Flathead

McDonald River

Josephine Lake

Grinnel Glacier

St. Mary Lake

Garden Wall

River

Avalanche Creek

Lake McDonald

Hanging Gardens

Cracker Lake

Chutes St. Mary

Sperry Glacier

Triple Divide

Jackson Blackfoot Glacier

Medicine Grizzly Lake

Going-to-the-Sun Road

Col. Pitamakan Pass

Two Medicine Lake

Glacier National Park

GLOSSARY/INDEX

OUZEL *31*—A small grey bird that dips and dives in streams searching for insects to eat.

PIKA *41*—A small, short-eared mammal that lives in rock piles or rock slides and gathers grass and other plants to dry for winter food.

PTARMIGAN *27, 41*—A bird that lives in alpine and subalpine areas and changes color from brown and white in summer to all white in winter.

ROCK FLOUR *31*—Powdered rock that has been ground up by a glacier and washes out of glaciers to color lakes and streams.

TUNDRA *5*—A cold, dry area where trees cannot grow, often found high on mountains.

U-SHAPED VALLEY *10*—A deep valley with a wide floor and steep walls carved by a glacier.